Welcome To

5 Minute Math

where fun and learning come together!

Hello 3rd grader!
We designed this book just for you! It was created to help you practice math skills that you will use in 3rd Grade. Plus, we added in <u>LOTS</u> of fun puzzles, challenges, and activities that we thought 3rd graders like you would enjoy! You'll find these on the back side of each practice page.

Enjoy!

Learner Tips

We added in some helpful reference pages towards the back of this book just in case you get stuck or want some visual examples.

These include:
- 2-D and 3-D Shapes
- Multiplication Strategies
- Multiplication Chart
- Fraction Examples
- Key Math Words
  (For addition, subtraction, multiplication, and division)
- Telling Time
- Place Value

We also added in some scratch paper towards the back of the book. You can use it for solving problems, creating your own puzzles and challenges, or just to doodle on!

BOOST
LEARNING

5 Minute Math Boost

Today I feel: ☺ 😐 ☹　　　Today is: S M T W T F S

Tap and Count: 10 20 30 40 50 60 70 80 90 100
Trace and Say: 10 20 30 40 50 60 70 80 90 100
Fill in the gaps: 10 ☐ 30 40 ☐ 60 70 ☐ 90 100

Add ⊕

20 + 10 = ___

50 + 10 = ___

Subtract ⊖

40 – 10 = ___

90 – 10 = ___

3-D Shape Match

● ● cone

● ● sphere

● ● cube

Compare

Which symbol goes in the circle?

> = <

97 ◯ 79

True or False

8+2 = 2+8

Circle: T or F

Place Value

What is the value of the 5?

752

Circle your answer:　500　50　5

A <u>quadrilateral</u> is any closed shape with 4 straight sides and 4 corners. <u>Circle all of the shapes that are quadrilaterals.</u>

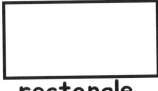
rectangle

triangle

trapezoid

square

Hidden Shapes

Can you find all of the hidden shapes in this picture?

| square | triangle | oval | trapezoid | circle | diamond |

5 Minute Math Boost

Today I feel: 🙂 😐 🙁   Today is: S M T W T F S

Tap and Count: 10 20 30 40 50 60 70 80 90 100

Trace and Say: 10 20 30 40 50 60 70 80 90 100

Fill in the gaps: 10 20 ☐ 40 50 ☐ 70 80 ☐ 100

Add ➕

70 + 10 = ___

90 + 10 = ___

Subtract ➖

70 - 10 = ___

40 - 10 = ___

3-D Shape Match

 • • cone

 • • sphere

 • • cube

Compare

Which symbol goes in the circle?

> = <

83 ◯ 65

True or False

7+3 = 10+0

Circle: T or F

Place Value

What is the value of the 3?

253

Circle your answer: 300 30 3

A <u>quadrilateral</u> is any closed shape with 4 straight sides and 4 corners. <u>Circle all of the shapes that are quadrilaterals.</u>

triangle

square

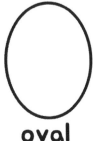
oval

trapezoid

Connect the Dots

Skip Count by 5's

SO COOL

Learner Tip:
Skip counting can help you learn your multiplication facts.

5 Minute Math Boost

Today I feel: 😊 😐 🙁   Today is: S M T W T F S

Tap and Count: 10 20 30 40 50 60 70 80 90 100

Trace and Say: 10 20 30 40 50 60 70 80 90 100

Fill in the gaps: 10 ☐ 30 ☐ 50 ☐ 70 ☐ 90 100

Add ⊕

20 + 10 = ___

10 + 50 = ___

Subtract ⊖

90 - 10 = ___

10 - 10 = ___

3-D Shape Match

 • • pyramid

 • • cone

 • • sphere

Compare

Which symbol goes in the circle?

> = <

46 ◯ 82

True or False

5+5 = 10+2

Circle: T or F

Place Value

What is the value of the 8?

Circle your answer:

800   80   8

A <u>quadrilateral</u> is any closed shape with 4 straight sides and 4 corners. <u>Circle all of the shapes that are quadrilaterals.</u>

trapezoid

pentagon

oval

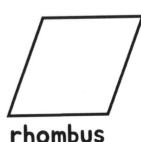
rhombus

Each character has a different value. Figure out how much each character is worth by solving the equations below.

🐱 + 🐱 + 🐱 = **15**

🐶 + 🐶 + 🐱 = **13**

🐵 + 🐶 = **14**

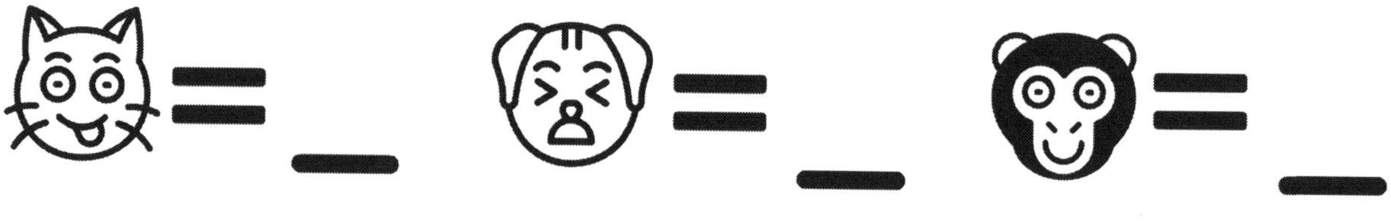

★★★★★★★★★★★★

🐱 = ___   🐶 = ___   🐵 = ___

5 Minute Math Boost

Today I feel: 😊 😐 ☹️   Today is: S M T W T F S

Tap and Count: 10 20 30 40 50 60 70 80 90 100

Trace and Say: 10 20 30 40 50 60 70 80 90 100

Fill in the gaps: 10 ☐ ☐ 40 ☐ ☐ 70 ☐ ☐ 100

Add ⊕

20 + 5 = __

25 + 5 = __

Subtract ⊖

35 - 5 = __

50 - 5 = __

3-D Shape Match

 • pyramid

 • sphere

 • cylinder

Compare

Which symbol goes in the circle?

> = <

39 ◯ 39

True or False

10+0 = 10-0

Circle: T or F

Place Value

What is the value of the 6?

603

Circle your answer: 600 60 6

A <u>quadrilateral</u> is any closed shape with 4 straight sides and 4 corners. <u>Circle all of the shapes that are quadrilaterals.</u>

trapezoid

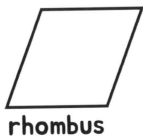
rhombus

pentagon

hexagon

Puzzling Patterns

Find each of these patterns in the grid below.

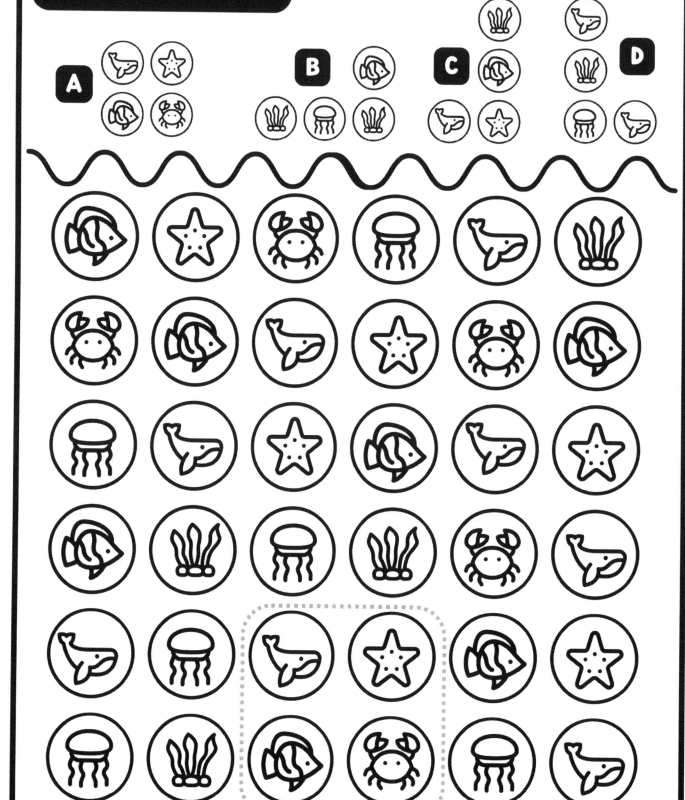

5 Minute Math Boost

Today I feel: 😊 😐 ☹️   Today is: S M T W T F S

Tap and Count: 10 20 30 40 50 60 70 80 90 100

Trace and Say: 10 20 30 40 50 60 70 80 90 100

Fill in the gaps: ☐ 20 ☐ ☐ 50 ☐ ☐ 80 ☐ ☐

Add ➕

40 + 5 = ___

55 + 5 = ___

Subtract ➖

65 - 5 = ___

80 - 5 = ___

3-D Shape Match

● ● pyramid

● ● sphere

● ● cylinder

Compare

Which symbol goes in the circle?

> = <

251 ◯ 125

True or False

10+5 = 15-2

Circle: T or F

Place Value

What is the value of the 4?

340

Circle your answer: 400 40 4

A <u>quadrilateral</u> is any closed shape with 4 straight sides and 4 corners. <u>Circle all of the shapes that are</u> <u>quadrilaterals.</u>

hexagon

rectangle

trapezoid

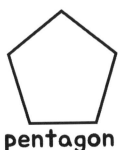
pentagon

Maze Time

Skip count by 10's to get through the maze and get to 100!

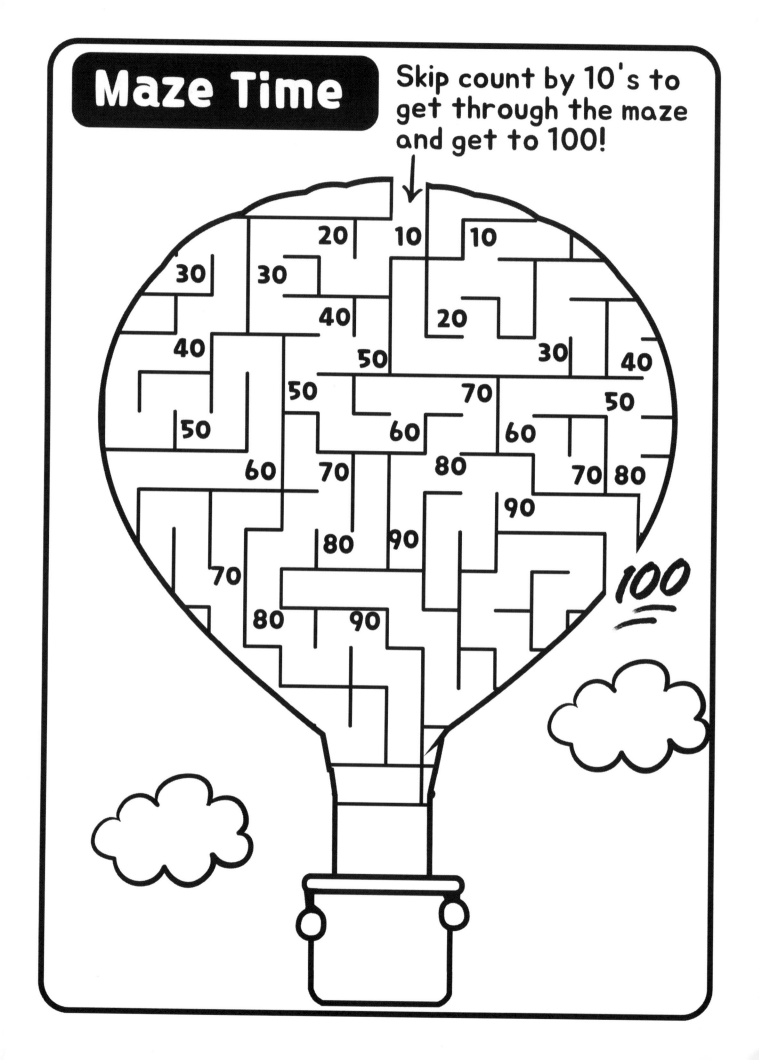

5 Minute Math Boost

Today I feel: 😊 😐 ☹️   Today is: S M T W T F S

Tap and Count: 5 10 15 20 25 30 35 40 45 50

Trace and Say: 5 10 15 20 25 30 35 40 45 50

Fill in the gaps: 5 10 ☐ 20 25 ☐ 35 40 ☐ 50

Add ➕

20 + 25 = __

65 + 15 = __

Subtract ➖

65 - 5 = __

80 - 5 = __

2-D Shape Match

 ●   ● pentagon

 ●   ● trapezoid

 ●   ● triangle

Quadrilaterals

Circle all of the quadrilaterals.

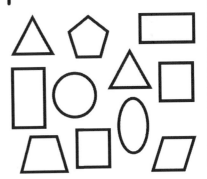

True or False

10+10 = 20-0

Circle: T or F

Expanded Form

Finish writing the number in expanded form.

235

200 + __ + 5

Multiplication as Repeated Addition

See the example below.

5 + 5 + 5 = (15)

We are adding the number 5 three times. So you see 5 three times which can be written as a multiplication problem that looks like this: 5 x 3 = (15)

Now you try it.

2 + 2 + 2 = (6)

2 x 3 = ( )

Triangle Teaser

How many triangles are there in this picture? Hint, there's more than 10!

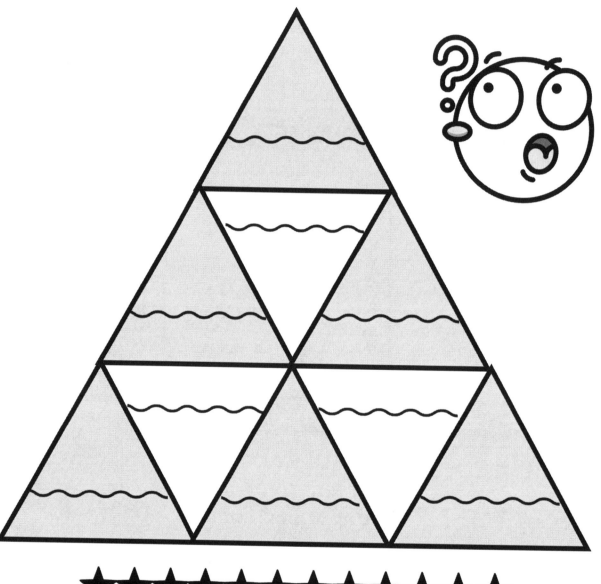

★★★★★★★★★★★★

_____ Triangles

5 Minute Math Boost

Today I feel: ☺ 😐 ☹   Today is: S M T W T F S

Tap and Count: 5 10 15 20 25 30 35 40 45 50
Trace and Say: 5 10 15 20 25 30 35 40 45 50
Fill in the gaps: 5 10 15 ☐ 25 30 ☐ 40 45 ☐

Add ⊕

25 + 25 = ___

90 + 10 = ___

Subtract ⊖

55 − 5 = ___

70 − 5 = ___

2-D Shape Match

 ● ● pentagon

 ● ● trapezoid

 ● ● triangle

Quadrilaterals

Circle all of the quadrilaterals.

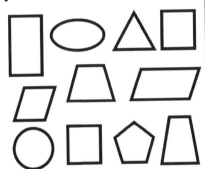

Number Guess

I am 7 <u>more</u> than 32. What is my number? ☐

Expanded Form

Finish writing the number in expanded form.

358

300 + __ + _

Multiplication as Repeated Addition

See the example below.

2 + 2 + 2 = 6

2 × 3 = 6

2 + 2 + 2 + 2 = 8

2 × 4 = _

3 + 3 = _

3 × 2 = _

Connect the Dots

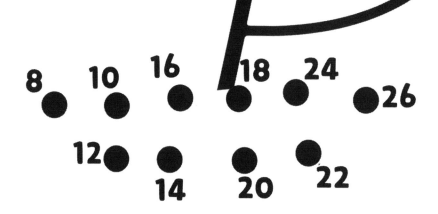

8   10   16   18   24   26

12   14   20   22

6   28

4   30

2   32

5 Minute Math Boost

Today I feel: 😊 😐 ☹️   Today is: S M T W T F S

Tap and Count: 5 10 15 20 25 30 35 40 45 50
Trace and Say: 5 10 15 20 25 30 35 40 45 50
Fill in the gaps: 5 ☐ 15 ☐ 25 ☐ 35 ☐ 45 50

Add ➕

50 + 25 = __

75 + 25 = __

Subtract ➖

90 – 5 = __

15 – 5 = __

2-D Shape Match

● ● oval

● ● trapezoid

● ● rhombus

Quadrilaterals

Circle all of the quadrilaterals.

Number Guess

I am 7 less than 32. What is my number? ☐

Expanded Form

Finish writing the number in expanded form.

708

700 + _ + _

Multiplication as Repeated Addition

5 + 5 = 10 → 5 x 2 = __

4 + 4 + 4 = 12 → 4 x 3 = __

3 + 3 + 3 = 9 → 3 x 3 = _

Shape Puzzle 1

How many of each shape do you need to make the dog? Hint, try drawing outlines around the shapes you find like we did for the face of the dog.

___ ___ ___ ___ 2 ___

5 Minute Math Boost

Today I feel: 🙂 😐 🙁   Today is: S M T W T F S

Tap and Count: 5 10 15 20 25 30 35 40 45 50

Trace and Say: 5 10 15 20 25 30 35 40 45 50

Fill in the gaps: ☐ 10 ☐ 20 ☐ 30 ☐ 40 ☐ 50

Add ➕

```
 25        75
+25       +23
----      ----
```

Subtract ➖

```
 75        84
-25       -23
----      ----
```

2-D Shape Match

- pentagon
- rhombus
- hexagon

Trapezoids

Circle all of the <u>trapezoids</u>.

Number Guess

I am 9 more than 63. What is my number? ☐

Expanded Form

Write the number in expanded form.

490

___ + __ + _

Multiplication as Repeated Addition

4 + 4 = _

⬇

4 x 2 = _

5 + 5 + 5 = __

⬇

5 x 3 = __

2 + 2 + 2 = _

⬇

_ x 3 = _

Number Sudoku

Fill in the boxes with numbers 1 – 4 so that in each row and each column the numbers are only used once.

3		1	
1	4	3	2
	3		1
2	1		

5 Minute Math Boost

Today I feel: Today is: S M T W T F S

Tap and Count: 2 4 6 8 10 12 14 16 18 20

Trace and Say: 2 4 6 8 10 12 14 16 18 20

Fill in the gaps: 2 4 6 8 ☐ 12 14 ☐ 18 ☐

Add

47   63
+32   +25
____   ____

Subtract

98   79
-64   -53
____   ____

2-D Shape Match

 •   • hexagon

 •   • pentagon

 •   • rhombus

Trapezoids

Circle all of the <u>trapezoids</u>.

Number Guess

I am 5 more than 78. What is my number? ☐

Expanded Form

Write the number in expanded form.

742

___ + __ + _

Multiplication as Repeated Addition

5 + 5 = __

_ x 2 = __

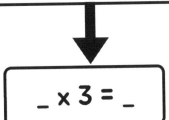
3 + 3 + 3 = _

_ x 3 = _

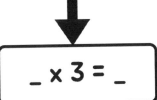
1 + 1 + 1 = _

_ x 3 = _

Addition Pyramid

When you add two numbers together on a lower row you will get the number above it.

5 Minute Math Boost

Today I feel: 😊 😐 ☹️   Today is: S M T W T F S

Tap and Count: 2 4 6 8 10 12 14 16 18 20

Trace and Say: 2 4 6 8 10 12 14 16 18 20

Fill in the gaps: 2 ☐ 6 ☐ 10 ☐ 14 ☐ 18 20

Fractions

Circle the answer for the fraction shown here.

$\frac{1}{2}$ $\frac{1}{3}$ $\frac{1}{4}$

Symmetry

Match the 2 halves.

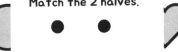

Pentagons

Circle all of the pentagons.

Number Guess

I am 3 less than 47. What is my number? ☐

Solve the Equations

Look for the addition or subtraction sign.

54
+35

42
+26

68
-25

Multiplication as Repeated Addition

Match the multiplication equation with the corresponding addition equation.

5 x 2   •   • 3 + 3 + 3 + 3

2 x 3   •   • 5 + 5

3 x 4   •   • 2 + 2 + 2

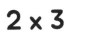

5 Minute Math Boost

Today I feel: 😊 😐 ☹️   Today is: S M T W T F S

Tap and Count: 2 4 6 8 10 12 14 16 18 20

Trace and Say: 2 4 6 8 10 12 14 16 18 20

Fill in the gaps: ☐ 4 6 ☐ 10 ☐ 14 ☐ 18 ☐

Fractions

Circle the answer for the fraction shown here.

$\frac{1}{2}$ $\frac{1}{3}$ $\frac{1}{4}$

Symmetry

Match the 2 halves.

Pentagons

Circle all of the __pentagons__.

Number Guess

I am 7 less than 92. What is my number? ☐

Solve the Equations

Look for the __addition__ or __subtraction__ sign.

$\begin{array}{r} 39 \\ +42 \\ \hline \end{array}$ $\begin{array}{r} 43 \\ +17 \\ \hline \end{array}$ $\begin{array}{r} 75 \\ -43 \\ \hline \end{array}$

Multiplication as Repeated Addition

Match the multiplication equation with the corresponding addition equation.

| 3 x 2 | • | • | 5 + 5 + 5 |

| 3 x 3 | • | • | 3 + 3 + 3 |

| 5 x 3 | • | • | 3 + 3 |

The numbers 0 through 9 are all hidden in this picture.
Can you find them all?

5 Minute Math Boost

Today I feel: 😊 😐 ☹️   Today is: S M T W T F S

Tap and Count: 2   4   6   8   10   12   14   16   18   20

Trace and Say: 2   4   6   8   10   12   14   16   18   20

Fill in the gaps: 2   4   ☐   ☐   10   ☐   14   ☐   ☐   20

Fractions

Circle the answer for the fraction shown here.

$\dfrac{1}{2}$ $\dfrac{1}{3}$ $\dfrac{1}{4}$

Symmetry

Match the 2 halves.

Hexagons

Circle all of the <u>hexagons</u>.

Number Guess

I am 5 less than 103 What is my number? ☐

Solve the Equations

$$349 + 32$$

$$527 + 41$$

$$495 - 43$$

$$752 - 80$$

Multiplication as Repeated Addition

Match the multiplication equation with the corresponding addition equation.

6 x 2	4 + 4 + 4
2 x 3	2 + 2 + 2
4 x 3	6 + 6

Color by Multiplication

Color by number multiplication style. Remember these two rules. Anything times zero always equals zero and anything times one is always the other number.

0 = blue
2 = red
4 = yellow

6 = pink
8 = brown
10 = gray

5 Minute Math Boost

Today I feel: ☺ 😐 ☹   Today is: S M T W T F S

Trace and Say: 2 4 6 8 10 12 14 16 18 20
Trace and Say: 5 10 15 20 25 30 35 40 45 50
Trace and Say: 10 20 30 40 50 60 70 80 90 100

Rounding

Round the number to the nearest 10.

57

_____

Fractions

$\frac{1}{2}$ • • ◔

$\frac{1}{3}$ • • ⊕

$\frac{1}{4}$ • • ◑

Hexagons

Circle all of the hexagons.

Symmetry

Is symmetry represented in this diagram?

Yes
No

Solve the Equations

825	768	567	842
+53	+23	-36	-23

Multiplication Chart

This is part of the multiplication chart shown on the back of this book. It can be used to help solve multiplication problems.

For example, 5 x 5 = 25. You go across on the 5 row and down on the 5 column. Where they intersect is your answer.
try this one on your own

2 x 3 = _

	1	2	3	4	5
1	1	2	3	4	5
2	2	4	⑥	8	10
3	3	6	9	12	15
4	4	8	12	16	20
5	5	10	15	20	㉕

Mystery Picture 1

Use the code below to color in the grid and find the mystery picture.

1	2	3	4	5	6	7	8	9	10
11	12	13	14	15	16	17	18	19	20
21	22	23	24	25	26	27	28	29	30
31	32	33	34	35	36	37	38	39	40
41	42	43	44	45	46	47	48	49	50
51	52	53	54	55	56	57	58	59	60
61	62	63	64	65	66	67	68	69	70
71	72	73	74	75	76	77	78	79	80
81	82	83	84	85	86	87	88	89	90
91	92	93	94	95	96	97	98	99	100

green

31, 40, 50, 60 70, 41, 51, 30, 91, 92, 93, 94, 95, 96, 97, 98, 99, 100, 1, 2, 3, 4, 5, 6, 7, 8, 9, 10, 61, 71, 81, 72, 82, 83, 18, 19, 20, 11, 12, 13, 21, 22, 79, 90, 88, 89

pink

53, 58

yellow

14 15 16 17 23 24 25 26 27 28 32 33 35 36 38 39 42 43 44 45 46 47 48 49 52 54 55 56 57 59 62 63 65 66 68 69 73 78 84 85 86 87

black

34, 37, 74, 75, 76, 77

5 Minute Math Boost

Today I feel: 😊 😐 ☹️   Today is: S M T W T F S

Trace and Say: 2 4 6 8 10 12 14 16 18 20
Trace and Say: 5 10 15 20 25 30 35 40 45 50
Trace and Say: 10 20 30 40 50 60 70 80 90 100

Rounding

Round the number to the nearest 10.

82

_____

Fractions

$\frac{1}{2}$ • •

$\frac{1}{3}$ • •

$\frac{1}{4}$ • •

Quadrilaterals

Circle all of the quadrilaterals.

Symmetry

Is symmetry represented in this diagram?   Yes   No

Solve the Equations

$$325 + 573$$ $$462 + 345$$ $$735 - 301$$ $$574 - 265$$

Multiplication Chart

This is part of the multiplication chart shown on the back of this book. It can be used to help solve multiplication problems.

For example, 3 x 3 = 9. You go across on the 3 row and down on the 3 column. Where they intersect is your answer.
try this one on your own

4 x 5 = _

	1	2	3	4	5
1	1	2	3	4	5
2	2	4	6	8	10
3	3	6	9	12	15
4	4	8	12	16	20
5	5	10	15	20	25

Puzzle Time

Each fruit has a different value. Figure out how much each fruit is worth by solving the equations below.

🍉 + 🍉 + 🍉 + 🍉 = 20

🍉 + 🍌 + 🍌 = 11

🍎 − 🍌 = 7

🍉 = __   🍌 = __   🍎 = __

★★★★★★★★★★★★

11	+	9	=	
+		+		+
18	+		=	24
=		=		=
	+		=	

17	+		=	
+		+		+
	+		=	13
=		=		=
23	+		=	45

5 Minute Math Boost

Today I feel: 😊 😐 ☹️   Today is: S M T W T F S

Trace and Say: 2 4 6 8 10 12 14 16 18 20
Trace and Say: 5 10 15 20 25 30 35 40 45 50
Trace and Say: 10 20 30 40 50 60 70 80 90 100

Rounding

Round the number to the nearest 10.

31

_____

Fractions

$\frac{1}{3}$ •   • ◐

$\frac{1}{4}$ •   • ◔

$\frac{1}{2}$ •   • ⊕

Quadrilaterals

Circle all of the quadrilaterals.

Symmetry

Yes
No

Solve the Equations

581	706	902	798
+235	+275	-471	-359

Multiplication Chart

Solve these equations using the multiplication chart as a guide.

2 x 4 = _

4 x 5 = _

5 x 3 = _

3 x 1 = _

	1	**2**	**3**	**4**	**5**
1	1	2	3	4	5
2	2	4	6	⑧	10
3	③	6	9	12	15
4	4	8	12	16	⑳
5	5	10	⑮	20	25

Color by Multiplication

Color by number multiplication style. Remember when multiplying by 2 you can just double the other number. You can also use skip counting by 2's to get to your answer.

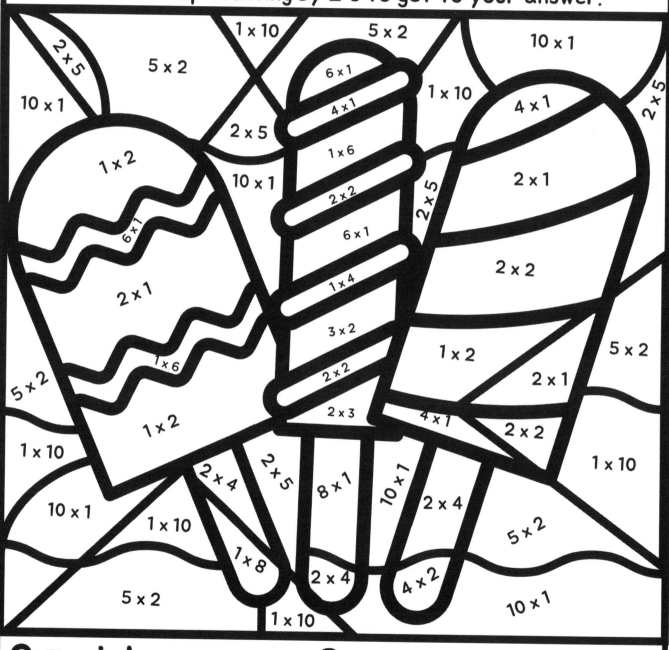

2 = pink
4 = green
6 = blue
8 = tan
10 = yellow

5 Minute Math Boost

Today I feel: Today is: S M T W T F S

Tap and Count: 3 6 9 12 15 18 21 24 27 30
Trace and Say: 3 6 9 12 15 18 21 24 27 30
Fill in the gaps: 3 6 9 12 ☐ 18 21 ☐ 27 ☐

Rounding

Round the number to the nearest 10.

75

_____

Fractions

$\frac{1}{3}$ •   •

$\frac{1}{4}$ •   •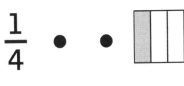

$\frac{1}{2}$ •   •

Octagons

Circle all of the _octagons._

Symmetry

Yes
No

Solve the Equations

| 925 | 608 | 732 | 803 |
| +438 | +237 | -257 | -492 |

Multiplication Chart

Solve these equations using the multiplication chart as a guide.

2 x 5 = _

3 x 2 = _

4 x 1 = _

5 x 4 = _

	1	2	3	4	5
1	1	2	3	④	5
2	2	4	6	8	⑩
3	3	⑥	9	12	15
4	4	8	12	16	20
5	5	10	15	⑳	25

Addition Magic Puzzles

Use the numbers given to help you solve the puzzles.
Add across and down to complete the puzzle.

2	+	3	=	
+		+		+
5	+	1	=	
=		=		=
7	+		=	

5	+	4	=	
+		+		+
5	+		=	7
=		=		=
	+	6	=	

4	+	5	=	
+		+		+
	+		=	
=		=		=
11	+		=	25

18	+	12	=	
+		+		+
	+		=	30
=		=		=
	+	22	=	

5 Minute Math Boost

Today I feel: 😊 😐 ☹️   Today is: S M T W T F S

Tap and Count: 3 6 9 12 15 18 21 24 27 30

Trace and Say: 3 6 9 12 15 18 21 24 27 30

Fill in the gaps: 3 6 9 ☐ 15 ☐ 21 24 ☐ 30

Rounding

Round the number to the nearest 100.

297

_____

Fractions

$\frac{1}{3}$ •   •

$\frac{1}{4}$ •   •

$\frac{1}{2}$ •   •

Octagons

Circle all of the <u>octagons.</u>

Symmetry

Yes

No

Solve the Equations

875	409	605	527
+693	+572	-428	-485

Multiplication Chart

Solve these equations using the multiplication chart as a guide.

	1	2	3	4	5	6	7	8	9	10
1	1	2	3	4	5	6	7	⑧	9	10
2	2	4	6	8	⑩	12	14	16	18	20
3	3	6	⑨	12	15	18	21	24	27	㉚

3 x 3 = _   2 x 5= _   1 x 8 = _   3 x 10 = _

Shape Puzzle 2

How many of each shape do you need to make this picture? Hint, try drawing outlines around the shapes you find like we did for the head of the fish,

5 Minute Math Boost

Today I feel: 😊 😐 😞   Today is: S M T W T F S

Tap and Count: 3 6 9 12 15 18 21 24 27 30

Trace and Say: 3 6 9 12 15 18 21 24 27 30

Fill in the gaps: ☐ 6 ☐ 12 ☐ 18 ☐ 24 ☐ 30

Rounding

Round the number to the nearest 100.

528

_____

Fractions

$\frac{1}{3}$ • •

$\frac{3}{4}$ • •

$\frac{1}{4}$ • •

Octagons

Circle all of the octagons.

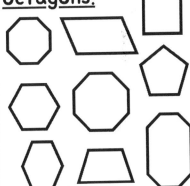

Symmetry

Yes
No

Solve the Equations

908	680	527	903
+425	+396	-295	-389

Multiplication Chart

Solve these equations using the multiplication chart as a guide.

	1	2	3	4	5	6	7	8	9	10
1	①1	2	3	4	5	6	7	8	9	10
2	2	4	6	8	10	12	⑭	16	18	20
3	3	6	9	12	⑮	18	21	24	㉗	30

3 x 5 = _   1 x 1 = _   2 x 7 = _   3 x 9 = _

Puzzling Patterns

Find each of these patterns in the grid below.

5 Minute Math Boost

Today I feel: 😊 😐 ☹️   Today is: S M T W T F S

3-D Shapes

How many faces does a cylinder have?

1
2
3
4

Money

What is the value of the money shown?

¢

Fractions

What fraction of the shape is shaded?

_____

Solve

$$536 + 705$$

$$325 + 498$$

$$849 - 368$$

$$906 - 794$$

Missing Addend

Fill in the missing numbers to make the equations true.

$50 + \boxed{} = 100$

$40 + \boxed{} = 100$

Written and Standard Form

Write these numbers in standard form.

| six hundred fifty one |

| nine hundred seventy eight |

651

_____

Multiplication Chart

Solve these equations using the multiplication chart as a guide.

$3 \times 5 = \underline{\ }$ $3 \times 10 = \underline{\ }$

$5 \times 2 = \underline{\ }$ $5 \times 6 = \underline{\ }$

$10 \times 4 = \underline{\ }$ $10 \times 8 = \underline{\ }$

	1	2	3	4	5	6	7	8	9	10
1	1	2	3	4	5	6	7	8	9	10
2	2	4	6	8	10	12	14	16	18	20
3	3	6	9	12	15	18	21	24	27	30
4	4	8	12	16	20	24	28	32	36	40
5	5	10	15	20	25	30	35	40	45	50
6	6	12	18	24	30	36	42	48	54	60
7	7	14	21	28	35	42	49	56	63	70
8	8	16	24	32	40	48	56	64	72	80
9	9	18	27	36	45	54	63	72	84	90
10	10	20	30	40	50	60	70	80	90	100

Hidden Symbols

Can you find all of the hidden symbols in this picture?

Bonus: Can you find 5 hidden numbers?

addition

subtraction

multiplication

division

less than

equal

greater than

5 Minute Math Boost

Today I feel: 😊 😐 😟   Today is: S M T W T F S

3-D Shapes

How many faces does a cone have?

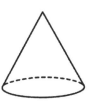

1
2
3
4

Money

What is the value of the money shown?

[ ] ¢

Fractions

What fraction of the shape is shaded?

_____

Solve

$$687 + 418$$

$$729 + 306$$

$$608 - 579$$

$$874 - 692$$

Missing Addend

Fill in the missing numbers to make the equations true.

$$52 + \boxed{} = 100$$

$$87 + \boxed{} = 100$$

Written and Standard Form

Write these numbers in standard form.

| eight hundred sixty two |

| one hundred seven |

862

_____

Multiplication Chart

Solve these equations using the multiplication chart as a guide.

$$2 \times 10 = \_$$

$$10 \times 10 = \_$$

$$8 \times 5 = \_$$

$$3 \times 7 = \_$$

$$6 \times 4 = \_$$

$$9 \times 1 = \_$$

	1	2	3	4	5	6	7	8	9	10
1	1	2	3	4	5	6	7	8	9	10
2	2	4	6	8	10	12	14	16	18	⃝20
3	3	6	9	12	15	18	⃝21	24	27	30
4	4	8	12	16	20	24	28	32	36	40
5	5	10	15	20	25	30	35	40	45	50
6	6	12	18	⃝24	30	36	42	48	54	60
7	7	14	21	28	35	42	49	56	63	70
8	8	16	24	32	⃝40	48	56	64	72	80
9	⃝9	18	27	36	45	54	63	72	84	90
10	10	20	30	40	50	60	70	80	90	⃝100

Be Creative

Draw your own video game scene that includes all of the shapes given.

5 Minute Math Boost

Today I feel: ☺ 😐 ☹   Today is: S M T W T F S

3-D Shapes

How many faces does a sphere have?

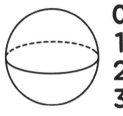

0
1
2
3

Money

What is the value of the money shown?

[____] ¢

Fractions

What fraction of the shape is shaded?

____

Solve

794
+508

945
+471

892
-275

500
-286

Missing Addend

Fill in the missing numbers to make the equations true.

[ ] + 43 = 100

79 + [ ] = 100

Written and Standard Form

Write these numbers in standard form.

| two hundred eleven | ____

| nine hundred eighty three | ____

Multiplication Chart

Solve these equations using the multiplication chart as a guide.

2 x 8 = _   8 x 10= _

7 x 3 = _   3 x 7 = _

6 x 9 = _   9 x 6 = _

	1	2	3	4	5	6	7	8	9	10
1	1	2	3	4	5	6	7	8	9	10
2	2	4	6	8	10	12	14	(16)	18	20
3	3	6	9	12	15	18	(21)	24	27	30
4	4	8	12	16	20	24	28	32	36	40
5	5	10	15	20	25	30	35	40	45	50
6	6	12	18	24	30	36	42	48	(54)	60
7	7	14	(21)	28	35	42	49	56	63	70
8	8	16	24	32	40	48	56	64	72	(80)
9	9	18	27	36	45	(54)	63	72	81	90
10	10	20	30	40	50	60	70	80	90	100

Color by Multiplication

Color by number multiplication style. Remember these two rules. Anything times zero always equals zero and anything times one is always the other number.

0 = purple
2 = green
3 = gray
4 = pink
5 = yellow
6 = blue

5 Minute Math Boost

Today I feel: 🙂 😐 🙁   Today is: S M T W T F S

3-D Shapes

How many faces does a cube have?

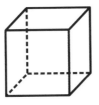

5
6
7
8

Money

What is the value of the money shown?

____ ¢

Fractions

What fraction of the shape is shaded?

_____

Solve

795
+386
____

572
+308
____

601
-342
____

700
-307
____

Missing Addend

Fill in the missing numbers to make the equations true.

☐ + 68 = 100

19 + ☐ = 100

Written and Standard Form

Write these numbers in standard form.

three hundred six

four hundred fifty seven

_____

_____

Multiplication Chart

Solve these equations using the multiplication chart as a guide.

5 x 8 = _

10 x 7 = _

2 x 6 = _

8 x 1 = _

3 x 4 = _

4 x 3 = _

	1	2	3	4	5	6	7	8	9	10
1	1	2	3	4	5	6	7	8	9	10
2	2	4	6	8	10	12	14	16	18	20
3	3	6	9	12	15	18	21	24	27	30
4	4	8	12	16	20	24	28	32	36	40
5	5	10	15	20	25	30	35	40	45	50
6	6	12	18	24	30	36	42	48	54	60
7	7	14	21	28	35	42	49	56	63	70
8	8	16	24	32	40	48	56	64	72	80
9	9	18	27	36	45	54	63	72	81	90
10	10	20	30	40	50	60	70	80	90	100

How Many?

How many rectangles can you find in this picture? Hint, there's more than 9!

_____ Rectangles

Odd one Out

Which emoji doesn't belong? Why?
There could be more than one correct answer.

1

2

3

4

5 Minute Math Boost

Today I feel: Today is: S M T W T F S

3-D Shapes

How many faces does a pyramid have?

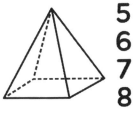

5
6
7
8

Money

What is the value of the money shown?

[ ] ¢

Fractions

What fraction of the shape is shaded?

_____

Solve

612
+597
_____

308
+507
_____

500
-299
_____

687
-425
_____

Missing Addend

Fill in the missing numbers to make the equations true.

[ ] + 98 = 100

19 + [ ] = 100

Written and Standard Form

Write these numbers in standard form.

eight hundred ninety six   _____

seven hundred fourteen   _____

Multiplication Chart

Solve these equations using the multiplication chart as a guide.

2 x 3 = _

3 x 2 = _

5 x 3 = _

8 x 2 = _

4 x 4 = _

9 x 5 = _

	1	2	3	4	5	6	7	8	9	10
1	1	2	3	4	5	6	7	8	9	10
2	2	4	6	8	10	12	14	16	18	20
3	3	6	9	12	15	18	21	24	27	30
4	4	8	12	16	20	24	28	32	36	40
5	5	10	15	20	25	30	35	40	45	50
6	6	12	18	24	30	36	42	48	54	60
7	7	14	21	28	35	42	49	56	63	70
8	8	16	24	32	40	48	56	64	72	80
9	9	18	27	36	45	54	63	72	81	90
10	10	20	30	40	50	60	70	80	90	100

Pathway Puzzle

Find the pathway that totals up to 50.

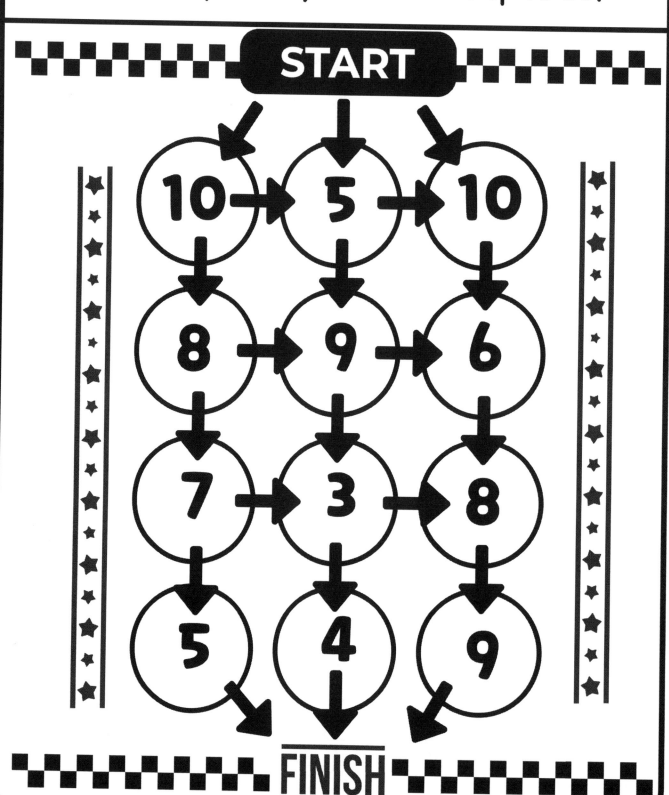

START

10	5	10
8	9	6
7	3	8
5	4	9

FINISH

5 Minute Math Boost

Today I feel: 😊 😐 ☹️

Today is: S M T W T F S

3-D Shapes

How many faces does a cube have?

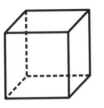

5
6
7
8

Money

What is the value of the money shown?

___ ¢

Fractions

What fraction of the shape is shaded?

_____

Solve

$$852 + 98$$

$$725 + 876$$

$$900 - 92$$

$$367 - 183$$

True or False

$$2 \times 3 = 3 \times 2$$

Circle: T or F

Written and Standard Form

Trace the number then write in in word form

257

302

Multiplication Chart

Solve these equations using the multiplication chart as a guide.

$3 \times 2 = \_$

$5 \times 3 = \_$

$10 \times 10 = \_$

$2 \times 3 = \_$

$9 \times 1 = \_$

$7 \times 5 = \_$

	1	2	3	4	5	6	7	8	9	10
1	1	2	3	4	5	6	7	8	9	10
2	2	4	6	8	10	12	14	16	18	20
3	3	6	9	12	15	18	21	24	27	30
4	4	8	12	16	20	24	28	32	36	40
5	5	10	15	20	25	30	35	40	45	50
6	6	12	18	24	30	36	42	48	54	60
7	7	14	21	28	35	42	49	56	63	70
8	8	16	24	32	40	48	56	64	72	80
9	9	18	27	36	45	54	63	72	81	90
10	10	20	30	40	50	60	70	80	90	100

Maze Time

Find your way through the maze of odd numbers.

YUM!

5 Minute Math Boost

Today I feel: ☺ 😐 ☹   Today is: S M T W T F S

3-D Shapes   Circle the cone.

Solve

852
+ 98
___

603
- 79
___

479
+ 25
___

Fractions

What fraction of the shape is shaded?

_____

Money

What is the value of the money shown?

 ¢

True or False

$5 \times 0 = 5 + 0$

<u>Circle</u>: T or F

Written and Standard Form

Trace the number then write in in word form

[   ]

[   ]

407

653

Multiplication Chart

Solve these equations using the multiplication chart as a guide.

$8 \times 1 = \_$

$6 \times 6 = \_$

$7 \times 4 = \_$

$8 \times 3 = \_$

$5 \times 7 = \_$

$4 \times 5 = \_$

	1	2	3	4	5	6	7	8	9	10
1	1	2	3	4	5	6	7	8	9	10
2	2	4	6	8	10	12	14	16	18	20
3	3	6	9	12	15	18	21	24	27	30
4	4	8	12	16	20	24	28	32	36	40
5	5	10	15	20	25	30	35	40	45	50
6	6	12	18	24	30	36	42	48	54	60
7	7	14	21	28	35	42	49	56	63	70
8	8	16	24	32	40	48	56	64	72	80
9	9	18	27	36	45	54	63	72	81	90
10	10	20	30	40	50	60	70	80	90	100

Mystery Picture 2

Use the code below to color in the grid and find the mystery picture.

1	2	3	4	5	6	7	8	9	10
11	12	13	14	15	16	17	18	19	20
21	22	23	24	25	26	27	28	29	30
31	32	33	34	35	36	37	38	39	40
41	42	43	44	45	46	47	48	49	50
51	52	53	54	55	56	57	58	59	60
61	62	63	64	65	66	67	68	69	70
71	72	73	74	75	76	77	78	79	80
81	82	83	84	85	86	87	88	89	90
91	92	93	94	95	96	97	98	99	100

yellow
71, 72, 81, 91, 83, 93, 85, 86, 95, 96, 88, 98, 79, 80, 90, 100,

black
34, 38

blue
2, 4, 5, 6, 7, 9, 13, 14, 15, 16, 17, 18, 22, 32, 25, 35, 26, 36, 29, 39, 51, 61, 52, 62, 59, 60, 69, 70

red
1, 3, 8, 10, 11, 12, 19, 20, 21, 30, 31, 40, 41, 42, 43, 44, 45, 46, 47, 48, 49, 50, 53, 54, 55, 56, 57, 58, 63, 64, 65, 66, 67, 68, 73, 74, 75, 76, 77, 78, 82, 92, 84, 94, 87, 97, 89, 99

5 Minute Math Boost

Today I feel: 🙂 😐 ☹️   Today is: S M T W T F S

3-D Shapes
Circle the sphere.

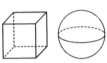

Solve

908	486	569
− 73	+ 71	+ 38

Fractions
What fraction of the shape is shaded?

_____

Money
What is the value of the money shown?

[   ] ¢

True or False

$7 \times 1 = 7 + 0$

Circle: T or F

Written and Standard Form
Trace the number then write in in word form

[   ]   811

[   ]   390

Multiplication Chart
Solve these equations using the multiplication chart as a guide.

7 x 3 = _	9 x 6 = _
5 x 6 = _	3 x 5 = _
8 x 1 = _	4 x 7 = _

	1	2	3	4	5	6	7	8	9	10
1	1	2	3	4	5	6	7	8	9	10
2	2	4	6	8	10	12	14	16	18	20
3	3	6	9	12	15	18	21	24	27	30
4	4	8	12	16	20	24	28	32	36	40
5	5	10	15	20	25	30	35	40	45	50
6	6	12	18	24	30	36	42	48	54	60
7	7	14	21	28	35	42	49	56	63	70
8	8	16	24	32	40	48	56	64	72	80
9	9	18	27	36	45	54	63	72	81	90
10	10	20	30	40	50	60	70	80	90	100

Puzzle Time

Each toy has a different value. Figure out how much each toy is worth by solving the equations below.

🏐 + 🏐 + 🏐 = 9

🪁 + 🏐 + 🪀 = 14

🪁 − 🏐 = 4

🏐 = _____   🪁 = _____   🪀 = _____

★★★★★★★★★★★★★

31	+		=	40
+		+		+
	+	5	=	17
=		=		=
43	+		=	

	+	35	=	45
+		+		+
14	+		=	
=		=		=
	+	56	=	

5 Minute Math Boost

Today I feel: 🙂 😐 🙁   Today is: S M T W T F S

3-D Shapes
Circle the cube..

Solve

$$725 + 82$$

$$602 - 53$$

$$413 - 392$$

True or False

$$5 \times 2 = 5 + 5$$

Circle: T or F

Money

What is the value of the money shown?

☐ ¢

Missing Numbers

Use skip counting and repeated additon to help you fill in the missing numbers on this part of the multiplication chart.

	1	2	3	4	5	6	7	8	9	10
1	1	2	3	4	5	6	7	8	9	10
2	2	4		8	10		14	16		20
3	3	6		12	15		21		27	30

Multiplication Chart

Solve these equations using the multiplication chart as a guide.

$$9 \times 5 = \_$$

$$3 \times 10 = \_$$

$$4 \times 1 = \_$$

$$7 \times 8 = \_$$

$$6 \times 8 = \_$$

$$2 \times 7 = \_$$

	1	2	3	4	5	6	7	8	9	10
1	1	2	3	4	5	6	7	8	9	10
2	2	4	6	8	10	12	14	16	18	20
3	3	6	9	12	15	18	21	24	27	30
4	4	8	12	16	20	24	28	32	36	40
5	5	10	15	20	25	30	35	40	45	50
6	6	12	18	24	30	36	42	48	54	60
7	7	14	21	28	35	42	49	56	63	70
8	8	16	24	32	40	48	56	64	72	80
9	9	18	27	36	45	54	63	72	81	90
10	10	20	30	40	50	60	70	80	90	100

Connect the Dots

Skip Count by 3's

Learner Tip:
You can use repeated addition. You just need to keep adding 3 to the last number.

5 Minute Math Boost

Today I feel: ☺ 😐 ☹   Today is: S M T W T F S

3-D Shapes Circle the cylinder.

Solve

```
  907          407          964
-  59        +  75        - 452
-----        -----        -----
```

True or False

$3 + 3 = 2 \times 3$

Circle: T or F

Money

What is the value of the money shown?

[   ] ¢

Missing Numbers

Use skip counting and repeated additon to help you fill in the missing numbers on this part of the multiplication chart.

	1	2	3	4	5	6	7	8	9	10
1	1	2	3	4	5	6	7	8	9	10
2	2		6		10		14		18	20
3	3	6	9		15	18		24	27	

Multiplication Chart

Solve these equations using the multiplication chart as a guide.

10 x 5 = _   8 x 3 = _

1 x 7 = _   6 x 4 = _

3 x 9 = _   8 x 8 = _

	1	2	3	4	5	6	7	8	9	10
1	1	2	3	4	5	6	7	8	9	10
2	2	4	6	8	10	12	14	16	18	20
3	3	6	9	12	15	18	21	24	27	30
4	4	8	12	16	20	24	28	32	36	40
5	5	10	15	20	25	30	35	40	45	50
6	6	12	18	24	30	36	42	48	54	60
7	7	14	21	28	35	42	49	56	63	70
8	8	16	24	32	40	48	56	64	72	80
9	9	18	27	36	45	54	63	72	81	90
10	10	20	30	40	50	60	70	80	90	100

Summer Sudoku

Fill in the boxes with numbers summer icon so that in each row and each column the pictures are only used once.

5 Minute Math Boost

Today I feel: ☺ 😐 ☹

Today is: S M T W T F S

3-D Shapes — Circle the pyramid.

Solve

$$423 - 152$$

$$503 - 62$$

$$721 + 386$$

True or False

$$3 \times 5 = 5 + 5$$

Circle: T or F

Money

What is the value of the money shown?

[   ] ¢

Missing Numbers

Use skip counting and repeated additon to help you fill in the missing numbers on this part of the multiplication chart.

	1	2	3	4	5	6	7	8	9	10
1	1	2	3	4	5	6	7	8	9	10
2	2				10				18	
3	3	6		12		18		24		

Multiplication Chart

Solve these equations using the multiplication chart as a guide.

2 x 9 = _

4 x 7 = _

6 x 3 = _

5 x 9 = _

7 x 10 = _

1 x 8 = _

	1	2	3	4	5	6	7	8	9	10
1	1	2	3	4	5	6	7	8	9	10
2	2	4	6	8	10	12	14	16	18	20
3	3	6	9	12	15	18	21	24	27	30
4	4	8	12	16	20	24	28	32	36	40
5	5	10	15	20	25	30	35	40	45	50
6	6	12	18	24	30	36	42	48	54	60
7	7	14	21	28	35	42	49	56	63	70
8	8	16	24	32	40	48	56	64	72	80
9	9	18	27	36	45	54	63	72	81	90
10	10	20	30	40	50	60	70	80	90	100

Odd one Out

Find the one that doesn't belong in each group.
There could be more than one correct answer.

1 2 3 5

After you find the one that you think doesn't belong.
Look again to see if you can come up with a different
answer. Ask someone else to play along and then
compare your answers.

5 Minute Math Boost

Today I feel: 🙂 😐 🙁　　　Today is: S M T W T F S

Shapes
Circle the 3-D shapes.
3-D shaspes are also called solid shapes.

Time
Write twelve thirty on the clock.

Elapsed Time
Zoe and her family went to the beach. They got there at 3:00 and stayed for 2 hours. What time was it when they left?

3:30
5:00
5:30
3:02

Money
What is the value of the money shown?

 ¢

Multiplication Chart
Fill in the missing numbers on the multiplication chart. Then solve the equations.

3 x 10 = _

9 x 5 = _

4 x 2 = _

3 x 8 = _

6 x 7 = _

7 x 6 = _

	1	2	3	4	5	6	7	8	9	10
1	1		3	4		6		8	9	10
2	2	4		8	10		14	16		20
3	3	6	9		15	18	21		27	
4	4		12	16		24	28	32	36	40
5	5	10		20	25	30	35		45	50
6	6	12	18	24	30	36		48	54	60
7	7	14	21	28	35		49	56	63	70
8	8	16	24	32	40	48	56	64	72	80
9	9	18	27	36		54	63	72	84	90
10	10		30	40	50		70	80		100

Multiplication Array
Another way of looking at multiplication is with an array. Looking at the example you can see that we have 2 rows with 3 dots in each row. So 2 x 3 = 6.

Now you try

Example
Row 1 ➡
Row 2 ➡
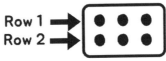
2 x 3 = 6

2 x 4 = _

3 x _ = 6

Color by Multiplication

Color by number multiplication style. Remember these two rules. Anything times zero always equals zero and anything times one is always the other number.

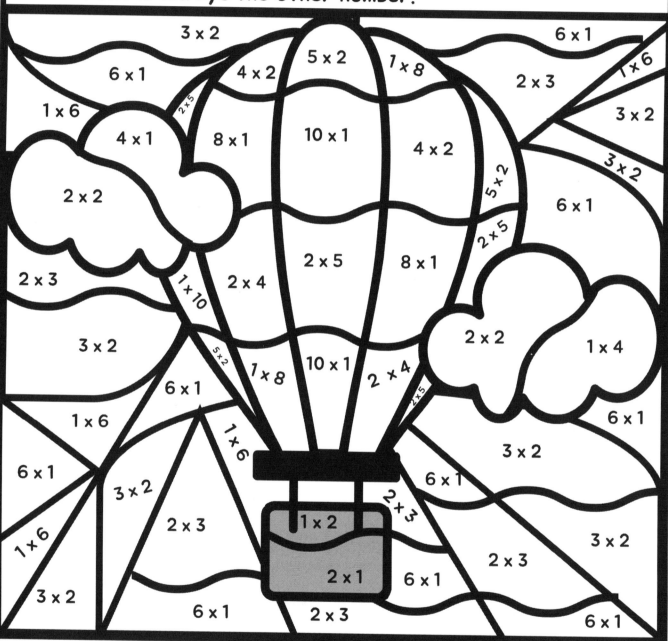

2 = gray
4 = white
6 = pink
8 = purple
10 = green

5 Minute Math Boost

Today I feel: ☺ 😐 ☹   Today is: S M T W T F S

Shapes

Circle the 3-D shapes.

3-D shaspes are also called solid shapes.

Time

Write two forty five on the clock.

Elapsed Time

Kayla and her friend went to the water park. They arrived at 11:00 and stayed for 3 hours what time was it when they left?

14:00
2:30
3:00
2:00

Money

What is the value of the money shown?

[ ] ¢

Multiplication Chart

Fill in the missing numbers on the multiplication chart. Then solve the equations.

7 x 6 = _

5 x 3 = _

4 x 10 = _

6 x 7 = _

8 x 5 = _

2 x 9 = _

	1	2	3	4	5	6	7	8	9	10
1	1	2		4	5	6	7	8		
2		4		8		12	14		18	20
3	3	6		12	15		21		27	
4	4		12	16		24	28	32	36	40
5		10		20	25	30		40		50
6	6	12	18	24	30	36	42	48	54	60
7	7	14	21	28	35	42	49	56	63	70
8	8	16	24	32	40	48	56	64	72	80
9	9	18	27	36	45	54	63	72	81	90
10	10	20		40	50		70	80		100

Multiplication Array

Solve each equation using the array as a guide.

2 x 5 = __

3 x 3 = _

4 x _ = 8

Secret Message

Use the secret funny bunny code to figure out the text message.

≋ = a
✿ = e
✦ = u
◎ = r
❀ = t
✳ = v
☀ = s
★ = H
⚡ = m
✩ = g

H A V E

A G R E A T

S U M M E R !

_ _ _ _
_ _ _ _ _
_ _ _ _ _ _ !

5 Minute Math Boost

Today I feel: 😊 😐 ☹️

Today is: S M T W T F S

Shapes
Circle the 3-D shapes.
3-D shaspes are also called solid shapes.
   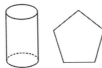

Time
Make the time on the clocks match.

Elapsed Time
Olivia and Sophie went to the carnival it was 1:30 when they got there and they stayed for an hour what time was it when they left?

2:30
3:00
2:00
1:31

Money
What is the value of the money shown?

¢

Multiplication Array
Solve each equation using the array as a guide.

2 x 3 = _

4 x 4 = _

Solve
Julia and her sisters picked plums from their grandpa's garden. Julia picked 68 plums, Josie picked 53, and Jayla picked 59. How many plums did the sisters pick altogether?

_____ plums

How many more plums did Jayla pick than Josie?

_____ plums

Shapes
What is the name of this shape? _____

Multiplication as Equal Groups
Equal groups is another way of looking at multiplication. Looking at the example you can see that there are 2 groups of 4. So, 2 x 4 = 8.

Example

2 x 4 = 8

Now you try

4 x 3 = __

Number Search

Find all of the numbers listed for each puzzle. The number can go left to right, up, down, or diagonal in any direction.

6	9	0	3	7
8	3	7	5	3
1	4	2	3	0
4	2	4	8	5
5	7	6	0	8

~~6903~~   7246
7305   3753
8353   7433
3288   7608
4473   4270

8	9	8	5	6
7	0	3	8	4
3	8	0	4	8
9	0	5	0	9
2	7	8	6	2

7038   9080
6048   8503
8000   9050
2008   8048
7856   9349

5 Minute Math Boost

Today I feel: ☺ 😐 ☹

Today is: S M T W T F S

Shapes
Circle the 2-D shapes.
2-D shapes are also called plane or flat shapes..

Time
Make the time on the clocks match.

7:30

Elapsed Time
Dusty and Devon went to the ice cream store. They left at 5:00 and we gone for 30 minutes. What time did they get back home?

5:30
5:03
30:05
9:00

Money
What is the value of the money shown?

 ¢

Multiplication Array
Solve each equation using the array as a guide.

1 x 5 = _   3 x 4 = _

Solve
Julia and her sisters sold plums for $3 per bag. If they sold 10 bags how much money did they make in total?

Plums for sale

$ _____

If Julia, Jayla, and Josie shared the money equally how much would they each get?

$ _____

Shapes
What is the name of this shape? _____

Multiplication as Equal Groups
Solve each equation using equal groups.

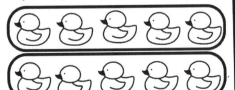 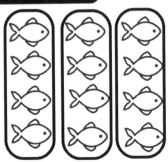 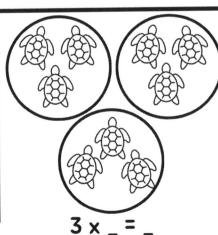

2 x 5 = __   3 x _ = 12   3 x _ = _

Find My Mate

Find the one that matches the item on the left.

5 Minute Math Boost

Today I feel: ☺ 😐 ☹   Today is: S M T W T F S

Shapes
Circle the 2-D shapes.
2-D shapes are also called plane or flat shapes..

Time
Make the time on the clocks match.

Elapsed Time
Alex and Brian went to pick blackberries. It took them 30 minute to pick them and they started at 11:30. What time did they finish?

12:03
2:00
11:33
12:00

Money
What is the value of the money shown?

 ¢

Multiplication Array
Solve each equation using the array as a guide.

_ x 5 = __

5 x _ = __

Solve
Xiomara went to the carnival she got to go on five rides. If each ride costs 2 tickets how many tickets did she use?

_____ tickets

Each carnival ticket costs $2. How much money did Xiomara spend on carnival tickets?

$ _____

Shapes
What is the name of this shape?

_____

Multiplication as Equal Groups
Solve each equation using equal groups.

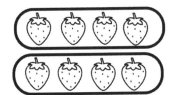

2 x 4 = _

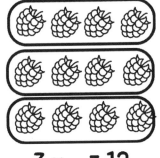

3 x _ = 12

3 x_ = __

You Create it - Mystery Picture

Use the 100's chart below to create your own mystery picture.

1	2	3	4	5	6	7	8	9	10
11	12	13	14	15	16	17	18	19	20
21	22	23	24	25	26	27	28	29	30
31	32	33	34	35	36	37	38	39	40
41	42	43	44	45	46	47	48	49	50
51	52	53	54	55	56	57	58	59	60
61	62	63	64	65	66	67	68	69	70
71	72	73	74	75	76	77	78	79	80
81	82	83	84	85	86	87	88	89	90
91	92	93	94	95	96	97	98	99	100

Write the code in here:

5 Minute Math Boost

Today I feel: 🙂 😐 🙁   Today is: S M T W T F S

Shapes
Circle the quadrilaterals.

Money
What is the value of the money shown?

 ¢

Time
Make the time on the clocks match.

Solve
Use one of the strategies you learned to solve these equations.

2 x 3 = _	5 x 9 = _	7 x 1 = _
4 x 5 = _	3 x 3 = _	2 x 8 = _

Division
Division is the opposite of multiplication.
When we divide, we split things into equal groups.

There are 5 in each of the 2 groups.

10 ÷ 2 = ⑤

Now you try
8 ÷ 2 = _

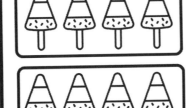

12 ÷ 3 = _

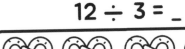

Using Data
Use the information in the chart to answer the questions.

Favorite Summer Activity

Swimming ||||| ||||| |||||

Hiking ||||| ||||

Rafting ||||

How many students participated in the survey? _____

How many students prefer swimming to rafting? _____

What was the least popular summer activity? _____

Puzzling Patterns

Find each of these patterns in the grid below.

A

B

  C

D

5 Minute Math Boost

Today I feel: 😊 😐 😞   Today is: S M T W T F S

Shapes
Circle the quadrilaterals.

Money
What is the value of the money shown?

 [___] ¢

Time
Make the time on the clocks match.

Solve
Use one of the strategies you learned to solve these equations.

$5 \times 3 = \_$ $8 \times 2 = \_$ $1 \times 1 = \_$

$3 \times 1 = \_$ $4 \times 3 = \_$ $2 \times 6 = \_$

Division
Division is the opposite of multiplication.
When we divide, we split things into equal groups.

$6 \div 3 = \_$ $15 \div 5 = \_$ $8 \div 2 = \_$

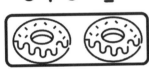  

Using Data
Use the information in the chart to answer the questions.

Favorite Carnival Treat

Snow Cone	𝍷𝍷𝍷𝍷𝍷 𝍷𝍷𝍷𝍷𝍷 IIII
Corn Dog	𝍷𝍷𝍷𝍷𝍷 𝍷𝍷𝍷𝍷𝍷 𝍷𝍷𝍷𝍷𝍷 II
Cotton Candy	𝍷𝍷𝍷𝍷𝍷 𝍷𝍷𝍷𝍷𝍷 𝍷𝍷𝍷𝍷𝍷 IIII

How many people participated in the survey? _____

What was the most popular carnival treat? _____

What is the total number of people who chose a sweet treat? _____

How Many Squares?

How many squares can you find in this picture?

Hint, there's more than 20!

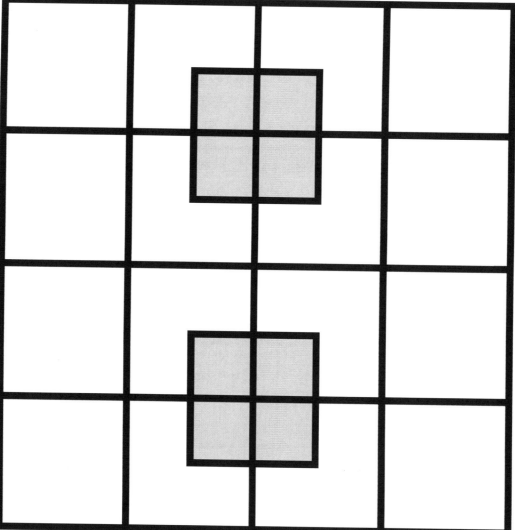

_____ Squares

5 Minute Math Boost

Today I feel: 😊 😐 😞   Today is: S M T W T F S

Symmetry

Does this show symmetry?

Yes

No

Money

What is the value of the money shown?

 ¢

Time

Make the time on the clocks match.

7 : 15

Solve

Use one of the strategies you learned to solve these equations.

4 x 3 = _	2 x 5 = _	7 x 5 = _
1 x 9 = _	3 x 4 = _	8 x 2 = _

Division

When we divide, we split things into equal groups.

$6 \div 2 = \_$

$20 \div 4 = \_$

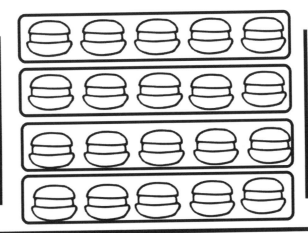

$5 \div 1 = \_$

Using Data

Use the information from the menu to answer the questions.

Snack Bar Menu

Snow Cone	$5
Corn Dog	$3
Cotton Candy	$4

Ava and her sister each got 2 corn dogs. Then they got some cotton candy to share. How much did they spend altogether?

$_____

If they had $20 to start with do they have enough money for each of them to get a snow cone?

Yes   No

5 Minute Math Boost

Today I feel: 😊 😐 😟   Today is: S M T W T F S

Symmetry

Does this show symmetry?

Yes

No

Money

What is the value of the money shown?

[____] ¢

Time

Make the time on the clocks match.

9 : 45

Solve

Use one of the strategies you learned to solve these equations.

| 5 x 3 = _ | 9 x 5 = _ | 2 x 7 = _ |
| 3 x 4 = _ | 4 x 1 = _ | 6 x 2 = _ |

Division

When we divide, we split things into equal groups.

9 ÷ _ = 3   _ ÷ 2 = 4

6 ÷ 3 = _

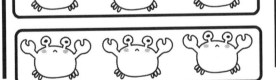

Using Data

Use the information from the menu to answer the questions.

Snack Bar Menu

Snow Cone $5

Corn Dog $3

Cotton Candy $4

If the snack bar sold 10 snow cones and 5 corn dogs in one hour how much did they make during that hour?

$ _____

If there are 24 corn dogs in a case how many would be left after that hour?

_____ Corn Dogs

Odd one Out

Find the one that doesn't belong in each group.
There could be more than one correct answer.

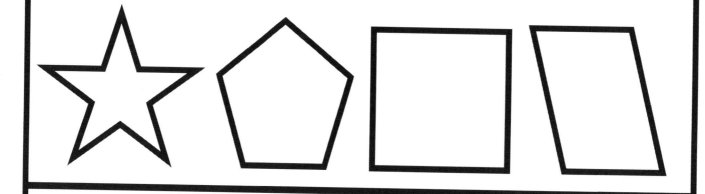

After you find the one that you think doesn't belong.
Look again to see if you can come up with a different
answer. Ask someone else to play along and then
compare your answers.

5 Minute Math Boost

Today I feel: Today is: S M T W T F S

True or False

4 x 2 = 4 + 4

True

False

Money
What is the value of the money shown?

[ ] ¢

Time
Make the time on the clocks match.

3 : 15

Solve
Use one of the strategies you learned to solve these equations.

9 x 2 = _   5 x 8 = _   7 x 5 = _

1 x 6 = _   3 x 3 = _   2 x 9 = _

Relating Multiplication to Division

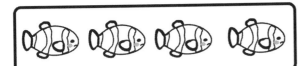

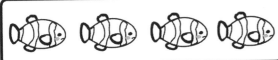

We have 2 groups of 4. This can be written in 2 ways.

2 x 4 = 8
8 ÷ 2 = 4

Now you try

3 x 2 = _
6 ÷ 3 = _

3 x _ = 9
9 ÷ 3 = _

Symmetry
Draw a line of symmetry for each of the items that you can. If you cannot show symmetry on that item circle it.

Puzzle Time

Each character has a different value. Figure out how much each character is worth by solving the equations below.

🐘 + 🐘 − 🦊 = **15**

🦊 + 🦊 + 🐁 = **12**

🐘 × 🐘 = **100**

🐘 = __   🦊 = __   🐁 = __

Help the dragon get to his friends.

Reference Pages

The following pages contain images and information that you can refer to as needed to help you complete the pages in this book. You can also save them and refer to them as a guide throughout your 3rd grade year and beyond.

We've also included scratch paper just in case you may need it for solving problems, creating your own puzzles and challenges, or just to doodle on.

If you found this book helpful or enjoyable please give us a rating or review and look for more books like this one from Boost Learning!

Scratch Paper

Shapes

3-D shapes are solid shapes

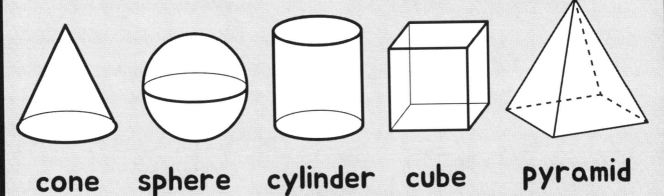

cone   sphere   cylinder   cube   pyramid

2-D shapes are flat shapes

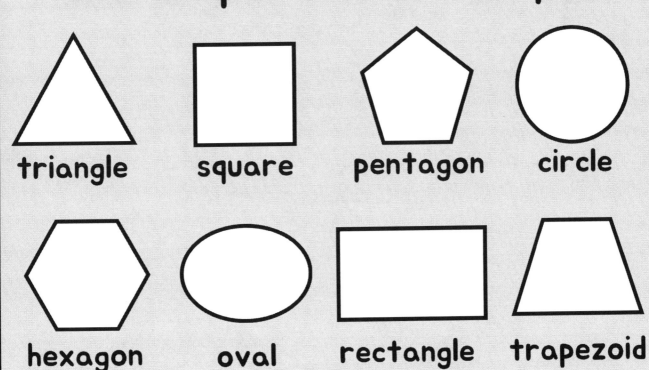

triangle   square   pentagon   circle

hexagon   oval   rectangle   trapezoid

Scratch Paper

Math Key Words

Math key words are certain words in a math problem that help tell you what math operation to use.

Addition

sum	altogether
add	how many in all
total	
plus	

Subtraction

difference	fewer
subtract	remaining
minus	

Multiplication

times
multiply
product
total

Division

divide
split equally
quotient
equal groups

Scratch Paper

Place Value

Place Value is the value of each digit in a number.

A 3 digit number has

Hundreds Place	Tens Place	Ones Place
5	**8**	**3**
5 Hundreds	8 Tens	3 Ones

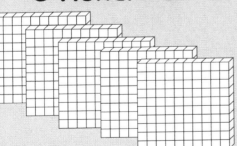
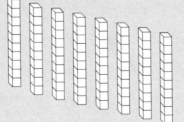

Scratch Paper

Fractions

Fractions are parts of a whole.

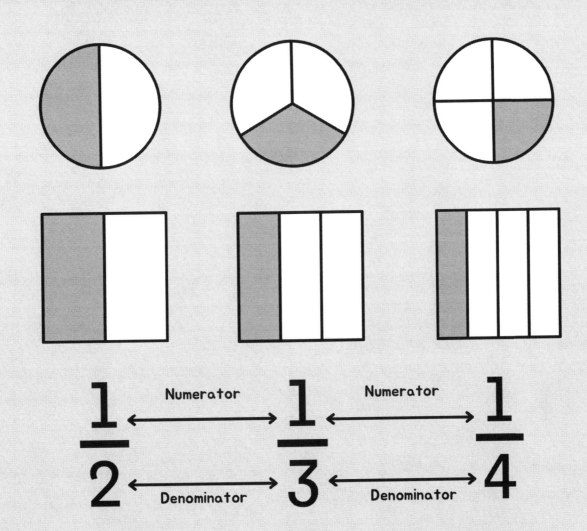

$$\frac{1}{2}$$ Numerator $$\frac{1}{3}$$ Numerator $$\frac{1}{4}$$

Denominator   Denominator

The bottom number of a fraction tells how many pieces the whole has been splint into. <u>The bottom number is called the denominator.</u>

The top number of a fraction is the part that is being referred to. In these examples it is the shaded part. <u>The top number of a fraction is called the numerator.</u>

Scratch Paper

Multiplication Chart

Explanation of how to use a multiplication chart

	1	2	3	4	5	6	7	8	9	10
1	1	2	3	4	5	6	7	8	9	10
2	2	4	6	8	10	12	14	16	18	20
3	3	6	9	12	15	18	21	24	27	30
4	4	8	12	16	20	24	28	32	36	40
5	5	10	15	20	25	30	35	40	45	50
6	6	12	18	24	30	36	42	48	54	60
7	7	14	21	28	35	42	49	56	63	70
8	8	16	24	32	40	48	56	64	72	80
9	9	18	27	36	45	54	63	72	81	90
10	10	20	30	40	50	60	70	80	90	100

Look at the numbers on the side of the chart. These are the rows. For this example we go to row 5.

Look at the numbers across the top of the chart. These are the columns. For this example we goto column 8.

in this example we go to row 5 and column 8. Where the row and the column meet is our answer.

5 x 8 = 40

Scratch Paper

Multiplication Tips

You can use any of these strategies to help solve a multiplication problem.

Repeated Addition	$2 + 2 + 2 = 6$ $2 \times 3 = 6$

Equal Groups	$2 \times 3 = 6$

Array	$2 \times 3 = 6$

You can use a multiplication chart.

Scratch Paper

Telling Time Tips
Analog Clock

The small hand points to the hour.

The big hand point to the minutes.

To count the minutes on the clock you can count through the 60 lines (tick marks). To count quicker, you can skip count by 5's.

When the big hand is on the 12 we say o'clock. In this example the time is one o'clock.

Scratch Paper

Scratch Paper

Made in the USA
Columbia, SC
10 August 2024

40284746R00057